LIVING WITH THE WILDFLOWERS

The pain and tears will be just a memory
Learn, grow, and heal from your darkest moments of despair.

Poems by

Tendai M. Shaba

LIVING WITH THE WILDFLOWERS

(The pain and tears will be just a memory)

Copyright © 2024 by Tendai M. Shaba.

Pachulu publishing.

From the author of Moments to Cherish (2020)

A lady in a Yellow Dress (2023)

For more information:

http://www.tendaishaba.com/

ISBN: 9789996083303

Find the sense of harmony and serenity within you.
Bask in the beautiful garden of tamed flowers. Your strength and will are strong.
Find the beauty in your imperfections and the nuances of life. Learn to live with the wildflowers too, representing the unpredictable nature of life's circumstances. Learn to unlock self-control in this unpredictable world. Believe in the glimpses of hope and acceptance. Unlock your strength to grow and heal from your darkest moments of despair, and all the pain and tears will soon be just a memory.

(Poems written from 2019 to 2023)

Table of Contents

Healing through words amid the wildflowers

Let me set you off on this healing journey through words and to address the loss of love and the loss of a loved one. I have lost. You have lost. We have all lost dearly on several accounts of our lives. I know what it feels like to have a mind filled with questions and to have a heart filled with pain. I have searched and searched for insight, clarity and direction to help heal my broken heart. As you read this, I want you to fathom the fact that others have stood where you stand now. They have experienced unbearable pain. They have reached the depths of despair. They too have been amid the wildflowers. I pray that you grasp the little light in the darkness and believe that your tears of pain will soon turn into tears of gratitude.

At this very moment, with a heavy heart, I miss my dearly departed younger sister Nomsa. She left this world so suddenly. It was painful watching her suffer in my eyes, and it was even more painful letting her go without saying goodbye.

I will always remember her bright smile and the joy she brought to my life and to all the other loved ones she cherished. As you read this book, painful and pleasant memories of people and everything you have lost will come. Do not be afraid. Consider these healing words part of your new, rich and fulfilling life. I pray that you grasp the little light in the darkness and believe that your tears of pain will soon turn into tears of gratitude.

Soon you will be looking back and all the pain and tears will be just a memory.

ALL THE PAIN AND TEARS

Leave it at the foot

Take the pain away, like weeds on the ground
It is yours to uproot
Take your anguish to God in prayer
Leave it at the foot
The foot of all grace, peace and light
Your pain is not all yours to fight
Trust in the purpose of your pain
And all your pain will wash away in the healing rain

Behind the smile

We all feel stressed, anxious
Frustrated and disappointed
We all go through difficult times
Those difficult times helped shape
Our way of thinking
Such as times of loss and failure
Those moments when we
Rediscover ourselves
Smiles where the pain is concealed
Hurt, anxiety, depression
And addiction, all concealed
I pray that we smile again
I pray that we heal behind the smile

Trapped in a forest of denial

Unexpected, the bad news you dreaded
Hearing the news that someone you love is dead
It courses straight to your brain
Like a speeding bullet aimed at your head
And the waves of shock course through your veins
When an angel dies, the tears pour like stormy rains
When love is lost, it's unbearable like labour pains
Acceptance sets you free from the shackles of despair, that
truth is inevitable
Those dark feelings are undeniable
You find yourself trapped in a forest of denial
Praying for deliverance and revival
Wishing for the trees to sing you a melody of peace
Hoping for your sadness to blow away like the wind at sea

Tormented

There will be wildflowers, expectedly
The memory flashes torment me
I ponder the question, how could this be
I broke something in anger, hurtful me
I wish I did something, regretful me
I wished it wasn't true, wishful me
I hoped you would make it, hopeful me
I prayed you would make it, prayerful me
In the end, you finished your story
The last page left me shocked and sorry
You are a book I revisit
To remember the sweetness of your love
The memories that calm me down and comfort me
Some memory flashes still torment me
But I have learned to appreciate the beauty of the tamed
flowers
And live harmoniously with the wildflowers

A chorus of weeps

I have heard the chorus of weeps
On that dark day, everyone hardly sleeps
The soul cries and the sadness peaks
The clouds fall and the denial speaks
The tears pour down and the pain creeps
In the aftermath of it all, the promise keeps
The hope rises and the faith leaps
This shall pass; peace comes to the one who seeks
With comfort and closure, the healing steeps
The nights get colder; it bleaks
I have heard the chorus of weeps

No schedule

Grief has no schedule
I love crying on a Sunday morning
You win when the tears stop, but there's no medal
On a steep road, this wagon of emotions has no brake pedal
I love relaxing on a Monday morning
You win when you avoid the stresses of the new week early
Climb to the peak, the mountain will deem you worthy
Your grief will fade away slowly and surely
The walls see me getting stronger daily

A million tears

I lent a million tears to the ocean
I have out-cried rivers
If I could live for a million years
Prayer would still be part of my devotion
If my sadness continues
Faith will still be my portion
I yearn to overcome; the pain will just be a notion
I trust the process, the healing is in motion
And when the inner peace finally settles, there will be no
commotion

I F

If I can catch a million teardrops
I can teach an eagle how to fly high
If I can catch a million teardrops
I can teach a river how to flow
If I can catch a million teardrops
I can reach out and touch the sky
If I can catch a million teardrops
I can teach flowers how to glow
My teardrops fall like stars
Each tear is a wish for peaceful days

Wisdom and strength

Now I know what it feels like to have a dagger in my heart
As the seasons come and go
I am devoted to a fresh start
After the pain and the tears
Comes wisdom and strength

Navigate some questions

My strength shall emerge
Now I know what it feels like to be hurt
Knowing that wildflowers are unpredictable
It's understandable, anything can trigger me
I shall not let the despair take control of me
If there's one thing about pain
It will have you sitting and contemplating
It will have you meditating and navigating
Provoking some questions to do with your faith and
spirituality
It will have you through a maze of heavy thoughts
And fluctuating emotions
I yearn to find the purpose of my loss
Time will heal me in due course

No pleasure in pain

There's no pleasure in pain
But, there is pleasure in dealing with the pain
Pain is intertwined with pleasure
You will have gloomy and sunny days
Times of joy and laughter are never far away
So much as April follows May
There are weeds for you to uproot
Where God has set for you to grow
Where God wants you to bear much fruit
Where God has planted you

Pain is inevitable

You will suffer and suffer for a little while
Pain is inevitable, never wonder why
You will weep and weep for a little while
Your tears will soon run dry

Suffering is optional

Dwell too much on the pain not
You will suffer in vain
And darkness will be your dominant thought
You will see longer and longer gloomy days
More and more gloomy days
Let sunny days be sunny days
Step into the light in your most cheerful way
Accept your pain and grow from it
Because pain is inevitable
And suffering is optional

God's promise

God promises that there is a purpose in pain
No pain is alike
We must all walk the path
That God has for our lives

Guilt and regret

I wish I could have saved you
That's my guilt and regret
I wish I responded to you every time you needed me
Every time you called
And every time you reached out
I can't begin to fathom the pain you were feeling
I was hopeful for your divine healing
That God places His healing hands upon you
So you could walk again and see another day
But God took away all your pain
He had a different plan for your life
Now you're in a better place
We miss you every single day

Denial into Acceptance

Turn your denial into acceptance
You have so many questions
And a heavy heart
Pondering will not do you any good
Turn your denial into acceptance
And leave your pain in the hands of God's deliverance

Strong faith over strong pain

My faith is stronger
Stronger than my pain
I believe in God and His deliverance
I cast all my worries and challenges
I increase my faith in the face of pain
Because my faith is stronger
Stronger than my pain

Rescue me

I cry for someone to rescue me
Rescue me from my gloomy days
To hold me
To listen to me
To cry with me
To suffer with me
To pray with me
And to fight with me
I deserve someone to rescue me
To be beside me on the sunny days
To smile with me
To laugh with me
To be joyful with me
To be cheerful with me
To be thankful to me
And to be prayerful with me
I cry for someone to rescue me
I deserve someone to rescue me

When the family grows

We thank God when the family grows
When the family portraits become bigger and bigger
And the smiles in the pictures become brighter and brighter
When our family bond grows stronger and stronger
We are in this together
Because it's not easy losing a family member
Letting go of the painful memories
And cherish the memories that brought so much joy into our
family

Widowed

Left all alone, I miss you dearly
I look to the heavens as you continue to rest
I am still thankful God brought us together
For all the precious moments
For all the time I experienced your undying love
It's not easy with you not being around
And every passing day I ask God for help
To help me through
Through my days without you
I ask God to cover me in the feathers of hope
To be under the wings of self-discovery
I look to the hills with teary yet joyful eyes
To turn my tears of pain into tears of gratitude
To find myself again
And to find peace and light

The loss of your love

The loss of your love
It follows me everywhere
From moment to moment
From room to room
From dream to dream
From thought to thought
From feeling to feeling
The pain of loss is unavoidable
I open myself to the pain, I am healable
I open myself to joy
To turn over a new leaf and be joyful

Over

I thought we would still be friends
That we would tie up the loose ends
We are over and done with, let's not pretend
Let's respect this, no room to resent

Near your broken heart

God is near to your broken heart
Urging you to move forward with your life
Helping you heal from the wounds
And comforting you
Your heart will be in the right place again
Soon

Rest

My mind can now rest
Set on resetting my heart
Love has put me to the test
I needed this rest
I was so hard-pressed
I felt the love pain in my chest
I was crushed
And I felt stuck
Now, I feel free
Set free from my main source of pain, you

Over again

I remember when it was clear that we were over
It felt like my heart was cut open
And was shredded into little pieces
Little pieces I have struggled to pick up
To piece together my heart so it can love again
You took my pride away
Like a broken pot that was once on display
We were really in love
Felt like we were meant to cross the bridge together
Now we're two perfect strangers
I wish you truly find what your heart desires
And I will do the same

Lock away

I want to lock away the unresolved feelings I have for you
And throw away the key
I want to let go
To reset my heart and set myself free
For now, my emotions are sealed
I will love and trust again until I am fully healed
To no longer feel trapped within
Let my healing process begin

Bitter

I wasn't always bitter
Someone made me this way
I wasn't always untrusting
Someone made me this way
I wasn't always fearful
Someone made me this way
I wasn't always uptight and resentful
Someone made me this way
I wasn't always this distant from love
Someone made me this way

Used to

It felt right, such a pleasant surprise
Remember when we used to
Watch the sunrise
It felt symbolic of our growing love
Now we watch it fade away
We used to make time for each other
Our connection was well-timed
Your love came to me just in time
We used to flock together
Seen everywhere, flock everywhere
Such lovebirds of the same feather
My tastes were your tastes
We used to talk all the time
Now we need others to talk to us
We used to be interested in our interests
Our plans and achievements
You lent me your love and I lent you mine
My debt of gratitude in parallel with yours
My decision-making in parallel with yours
My choices in parallel with yours
Now it feels like
We're heading in opposite directions
We used to celebrate each other
Now we have to remind each other of our special dates
I hope it is not too late to rekindle our love
To once again drink from the well of love
Because we used to love each other well

Forgotten

I have forgotten my importance

Another day to wallow

Another day to suffocate, slowly losing my breath

In my state of emptiness

I have forgotten my purpose

Surely, this can't be life

This can't be life

I pray to find the peace of mind I seek

So I no longer hide behind my smile

Stronger and pure

You took my sweetness for weakness
Sadly, I have accumulated all this bitterness
I have dug deeper to find myself
To find what makes me truly happy
To forgive and forget
My past is my past
Love, it now lodges in my heart
My mind is set on peace
My spirit basks in the light
And my faith is stronger and pure

Love wins

Let us remember the loved ones we've lost
We miss them
We cherish their memories
They are forever in our hearts
Love wins and God is love

Poem cry

I feel deep sadness inside my heart
So I have to make this poem cry
See the tears coming down my eyes
So I have to make this poem cry

Empty

Empty is how I feel
When all meaning is lost
And all that is left is a wandering soul
A broken spirit
And a mind infested with emptiness
May I return to a path of spirituality?
A path of soulfulness
So I feel fulfilled
And no longer feel empty

Check on me

I have my worries
I have my doubts
Check on me
Once in a while
Just so I can remember
What it means to have you as my friend
I have my fears
I have my misfortunes
Check on me
Once in a while
Just so I can remember
What it means to have you as my friend
And to all my friends
Check on your friends
Mental exhaustion is real

Holding back tears, weeping inside

Unless you have had that experience before
Don't say, "I know how you feel"
Because you don't
Because you don't
People you think are the strongest
Are the ones holding back tears and weeping inside
They need you to brighten up their day
Put your arm around them
They need you to open up
So they too can open up

Certificate of fitness

You caught me
Guilty as charged
My problem is my spiritual health
My relationship with God
A health issue
Because I have been unfit for a while
Consumed by fear and anxiety
So I pray to my glorious God
Restore my mind to a mind of glory
A mind fit to bask in your glory, God
Restore me to a person of glory, God
A person fit to bask in your glory, God
Help me grow from these dark days
And dark moments
The time has come
To renew my certificate of fitness

As a waning moon

I have seen growth
I have seen a change
I have seen a renewal
I have seen beauty
I have seen a new moon
I have felt love
I have felt the rain
I have felt all kinds of energy
I have felt pain
I have experienced dark days and dark moments
I have felt anxious and depressed
But one truth remains, that time is precious
That I will not lose my light as a waning moon
And that God will never leave my side

Suddenly

I guess I never knew the pain
The heartbreak
My heart will never be the same
When God called out your name
You are now in a peaceful place, no more pain
I need all the scripture to comfort me
How could you leave so suddenly?
We will all miss you
And all I remember is your smile

I will be fine

Amazed by how I never saw you frown
You always stretched your hand to all who needed you
You were heaven-sent, such an angel
What a life, what a soul
Gone but forever in our hearts
I am learning how to smile again
And how to laugh again
Father stretch your healing hand
Help me to believe again
Wipe the tears in my eyes
And I will be fine

Single

I am on a path of self-discovery
To discover my smile
And what makes me happy
To discover my thoughts and feelings
My fears and doubts
My choices and decisions
To learn to walk alone
Before I learn to walk with someone else
Before I share my life and time with someone else
I pray that God teaches me how to love
How to trust, to be faithful
How to give, how to share
How to forgive, how to listen
And how to commit
I believe in love
And love is a beautiful thing

God knows

God knows why we separated
Why we grew apart
Sometimes I wonder
Why did He let you depart?
Loss has taught me how to rediscover myself
Moving on, growing and letting go
And I thank God that I'm still here
With a heart full of love
With so much love to give
I've learned to love again, to believe again
And to trust again
Because God is always showing me, love
I believe in love
And love is a beautiful thing

Numb

I have been on a journey
On a journey to realize oneself
To realize oneself, to grow with God
So I no longer feel numb
Because sadness makes me numb
Disappointments make me numb
Frustrations make me numb
Pretence makes me numb
Isolation makes me numb
Smiling when it hurts makes me numb
But I pray
I pray to reclaim my life
So I no longer feel numb

We wish we had more time with you

Our dearly departed
We still remember
Our hearts still bleed
Our lips still question
How you departed, so suddenly
God knows, we still cherish your memory
We were too young to understand
But we are so grateful now
To have had an angel like you
In spirit, you have been in our lives
You continue watching over us
We accept
As God continues to heal our hearts
To work hard and make you proud
So we find peace in our hearts
We wish we had more time with you
Continue resting in peace
We love you

Flip the pages

As we continue to flip the pages
On this journey full of promises from chapter to chapter
A promise that gives and takes away
A promise of pleasure and pain
A promise of high highs and low lows
Such a beautiful promise, full of life

The promise

A promise to witness the sunrise and sunset
Another chapter to ponder the question
What is my true purpose?
What is my true identity?
Where do I belong?
Who do I love?
Where do I go?
How do I get there?
Which is the right path?
I am truly
Searching for the true meaning of my life

Gallery

My Gallery
The keeper of my beautiful treasures and precious memories
The cheerful memories that bring instant joy
And the painful memories that strengthen my day
I keep all these things that are so dear to my heart

Ashes

This flower that once was
A symbol of love, now a dead flower
The flames came and went
Now all that is left are ashes
The ashes of happiness, once upon a time
Amicably or not
These ashes now symbolize
The pain and suffering
The loss of something that was once good
The ashes of something that was once one flesh
The ashes of the lost love and respect
There's no room for reconciliation
But there's room for self-restoration
And watching the ashes blow away in the wind

Receive my hug

I'm fond of your pleasantness
I feel compassion when I see you
Upon your presence
My reaction is to embrace you
My hug is a gesture
Of me pouring love into your heart
If you're in any pain
My warm hug is your painkiller
If you're hurting
You can cry on my shoulder
If your spirit is crushed
My hug is there to comfort you
I appreciate you deeply
Feel the bond of our trust and the honesty between us
Receive my hug with open arms

God has a plan for you

Start your day right
Have faith, fight a good fight
Have your mind suppress the pain
Speak your mind and address the pain
Under stress, you deserve a rest
Retreat and meditate, time to reflect
Make no mistake, learn from your mistakes
At the end of the day, it's your choices
Your decisions and your voice
Strive to be better, strive to do better
Note to self, this is your letter
To motivate you to be a goal-getter
To get your happiness
To get your good health
To get your hands on your future
And to get your wealth
God has a plan for you

Forgive me

If I ever wronged you in any way
Forgive me, I'm sorry
If I ever caused you any pain
Forgive me, I'm sorry
As I continue to learn from my mistakes
As I continue to grow from my mistakes
If I was ever the cause of your worries
Forgive me, I'm sorry
If I was ever the cause of your misfortunes
Forgive me, I'm sorry
As I continue to learn from my mistakes
As I continue to grow from my mistakes
Find it in your heart to forgive me
As I also learn to forgive myself

A baby lost

I was ready for you
We were ready for you
To welcome you into our home
And give you warmth in this cold world
I was ready to carry you
We were ready to carry you
Felt you growing big
Bigger and bigger till the day you finally arrive
I feel the pain
We feel the pain
God knows this story is untold
He has all the answers to our questions
Why we won't get to finally carry you
And why we won't get to finally meet you
Our hope and faith remain intact
God is good
And God knows best

Day 1: the wave of shock

When the wave of shock hits
One that crushes your heart and soul into bits
Hard to process what you just heard or saw
Experiencing such a pain you have never felt before

Day 2: struggling to make sense of it all

Struggling to make sense of it all
To navigate through it all
To live through it all
And to survive through it all

Day 3: standing over this dark cloud

Standing over this dark cloud
Still trying to process this dark moment
Still wearing this frown
I am haunted with unrelenting torment

Day 4: lost and hopeless

I feel lost and hopeless
I need to be embraced, I need solace
I have never been this cheerless
I will smile again, that is my promise

Day 5: lingering in the shadows

I am the one lingering in the shadows, the silent mourner
The whispers of pain are all I hear
I am that haunted house by the corner
At this moment, no one is welcome here
My soul is a dark window, succumbed to fear

Day 6: the faint glimmers of hope

The faint glimmers of hope
Become fainter and fainter
The pillars of my faith
Become weaker and weaker
The grounds of my joy
Become shakier and shakier
The light of my soul becomes darker and darker

Day 7: reset my heart again

I am defeated by overwhelming emotions
The wings of hope carry all my devotions
Trying to find my way again
I have loved and lost
Trying to reset my heart again

Day 8: it can't be

It can't be
You were here with me just yesterday
It can't be
We were laughing together just yesterday
It can't be
We were talking just yesterday
It can't be
You were full of life just yesterday

Day 9: beyond my control

I wish I could fix this
But it's beyond my control
All I can do is
Remember the love you showed me
And the love I showed you
That is all I can control

Day 10: gone like the wind at sea

I refuse to believe you are gone
Gone like the wind at sea
I have endless questions that I need endless answers to
Like how could this be?
The pain is unbearable; at least I open my eyes to see
You are gone but your memory will always remain with me

Day 11: I found my smile again

I found my smile again
I am grateful and free
Being as understanding as I can be
I can smile again

Day 12: the wings of hope

The wings of hope carry all my devotions
I believe in the powerful purpose of prayer
I welcome the brighter days
I believe in a new and fulfilling life

Day 13: purpose in life

I believe in my purpose in life
There's a reason I am here
I believe in my power to bring light to others
There's a reason I am here

Your date of birth number matters: 1-9

To new beginnings and new hope
To spiritual guidance and growth
God sets me in the right direction
To remind me that I am not alone
My hopes and dreams are in the hands of God
To find purpose, and balance and to fly high
To live, to pray, to play, to laugh and to cry
In God, I find stability
I find the strength to grab every opportunity
To be soulful and focus on my spirituality
To follow my heart and to be selfless
To feel complete
Because I feel complete with God in my life

Your date of birth number matters: 10-16

To feel complete and stable
To do all I can do
To be all I can be
To remember God because He never forgets me
I believe in God
Who protects and blesses me
Who gives me opportunities and second chances
A God who makes all things happen
I embrace my flaws and insecurities
Because that's how I find growth and change
I pray to make better choices and decisions
My prayers are powerful
And I learn from my mistakes
I pray to feel complete
Because I feel complete with God in my life

Your date of birth number matters: 16-23

To have a great character
Attitude and mentality, I believe in a great God
To find my purpose, I believe in a great God
To find happiness, I believe in a great God
To find abundance, I believe in a great God
I am thankful
Because I believe in a great God
To surround me with love and light
To keep going with all my might
My hopes and dreams are great
My potential is great
All because I believe in a great God
To focus on my progress in life, to grow
And to feel complete
Because I feel complete with God in my life

Your birth date number matters: 23-31

To focus on being kind and generous
Being thoughtful and gracious
I believe in God, I believe in oneself
And I believe in others
I have a big heart and open arms
My thoughts and ideas become
Because God blessed me with a vision
To pray for every choice and decision
God gives me power and purpose
Because God believes in my potential
To think and see things differently
To face all life challenges strongly
To work hard with all my might
Because good things will come
To be joyful and feel encouraged
To be hopeful and feel motivated
Because God is with me, I am never alone
To move forward and be transformed
To be complete
Because I feel complete with God in my life

WILL BE JUST A MEMORY

Memories will linger on

At this very moment, I start looking back
It's never easy to say goodbye
But these memories will linger on as time goes by
To turn my tears of pain into tears of gratitude
To find strength in my period of spiritual solitude
To free oneself from the tight grip of denial
A true test of my faith, this is just another trial
This is my acceptance of the inevitable truth
To set myself free, my soul shall be soothed
In faith, my suffering is not in vain
These memories will linger on; I will grow from my pain

God is bigger than your problems

Your God is bigger than your problems
Your problems are not bigger than your God
Your God is bigger than your worries
Your worries are not bigger than your God
Your God is bigger than your fears
Your fears are not bigger than your God
Your God is bigger than your pain
Your pain is not bigger than your God

The echoes of farewell

Gone from our sight, but at home in our hearts
Your memories will never fade away
We cherish your memories each passing day
We light candles and illuminate our hearts
Honoring the lives of loved ones
The lives of the dearly departed
The grandfather, the grandmother
The father, the mother
The brother, the sister
The husband, the wife
The uncle, the aunt
The baby, the child
And the friend
These are the echoes of farewell
We miss them, we let love prevail

The sweetness of your love

I will fill my heart with love
And with the most beautiful flowers from the garden of
nostalgia
Without the breath of your love
Your absence is my asthma
The winds echo with whispers from my wounded soul
Without you
I am merely a lonely night without the moon and stars
Still, I remember
The sweetness of your love for me
And my undying love for you

Wildflowers

When my thoughts and feelings become untamed as
wildflowers
My garden of hope will truly reflect my resilience
And the beauty of my imperfections
I embrace the beauty of these wildflowers
I understand the language of pain, inked in tears
I understand getting burned; nearing a fire is one of my fears
These wildflowers are untamed
They truly define the depth of my pain

A c c u s t o m e d   t o

The tears are my pain's true reflection
Letting go of the love I am accustomed to
Letting go of that deep connection
As I mop my tears and mend all the broken pieces
Treat all the parts that ache and tear
I will not let fear break me into little pieces
I will let go of the love I was accustomed to
Let go of the deep connection
The comfort and affection
The loss of a loved one and the love they give are heavy
I will rise from the deep shadows of the pain so I no longer feel
empty

Healing along the way

This is my time to heal, no more excuses
There will be bumps
There will be bruises
I will hear the silent whispers
I will see the flashes
There will be reminders
There will be pauses and dashes
This is my time to heal, no more excuses

Set my fire of hope

Healing along the way will set my fire of hope
I will light up the match, I will cope
Through the dark valleys, I will go
Face to face with fear, I will show
That I am strong
That I will not sink into the depths of despair
And when the new and bright sunny day comes
I will be there

The sky cries with me

You will not see my tears in the rain
But they will run down my cheeks
I release the pain when I weep
And the sky cries with me
I believe in a sunnier tomorrow
I believe in shared sorrow

A broken bone

If a broken bone heals
Definitely, my broken heart can heal
I long for this simplicity
But I know how complex matters of the heart are
Resetting my heart and looking forward
With a mended heart I will go far

The sweetness of love

I live for the sweetest of love
As if my heart pumps honey
The kind of love that is spirited and sunny
I live for the richness of love
Coursing through my veins
The kind of love that kills my pains
The kind of love that pushes me
The kind of love that pulls me back
Moving forward with strength
Mending my broken heart
For a new and fulfilling life
I will go the length
Believing in the transformative power of healing
Moving forward is my everyday feeling
I will brave the sticks and stones
Knowing that emotional wounds are not broken bones
This healing journey takes time, that's the magnitude
I will turn my tears of pain into tears of gratitude
I will pray that my feelings shall be resolved
I will remember the sweetness of the love that I give
And I will remember the sweetness of the love that I lost

When the angels cry

When the angels cry, it rains
When the tears drop, it pains
The emotions become heavy, it drains
The shadows become thicker, it chains
The nights become colder, it sustains
The belief of a sunny day, it remains
My hope for a better tomorrow, it gains
And my belief in divine power, it remains

Take me as I am

My trust, take it
My faith, take it
This is my reverence for something bigger
This is my deliverance for something bigger

There will be tears and pain

The inevitable truth remains
There will be tears and pain
There will come a time when we fall to the depths of despair
There will also come a time when we climb up the stairs

Fail

Fail
Not because you don't have hope
Not because you don't have faith
Not because you don't have the passion
Not because you don't have the support
Fail because you try
Fail because you learn from failure
Fail because you understand
That to fail is to become
Understand that your winning moment will come

Living with the wildflowers

With everything you face
Embrace it with grace
All the tears will wash away in the rain
And all the pain will soon be just a memory
You believe that if a broken bone can heal
Your broken heart can heal too
You know what it means to feel blue
But you are strong and inspired
You are beautiful and admired
Beauty, love, peace and light surround you
As a loss, sadness, fear and anguish do too
You acknowledge all the wildflowers
You accept all the wildflowers
And you find peace living with the wildflowers

Grace

I have walked into rooms before
All odds against me
In the face of staring eyes and whispering lips
My only hope and prayer
If God is for me, who can be against me?
Against all odds
I push until something happens
I pray until something happens
It might not happen today
But God gives me strength
My strength is faith and faith is my strength
I have faced so many doors slamming shut in my face
I never lose hope
Because God will open another door for me
And that is God's grace

Important you

Be important
Let them remember your importance
Let them reward your importance
Let them praise your importance
Nice moments are forgettable
Build important moments
Unforgettable important moments
Things you did
Things you said
You are important, they feel your impact
Don't be afraid to show your importance
Important you

In no particular order

Make plans
Make moves
Help myself
Help others
Thank God
Thank family
Thank friends
Live a little
Live abundantly
Have an abundant life
Laugh, cry
Fall, fail
I love my life
Gaining strength and wisdom as I get older
All that, in no particular order

Courage

You found the courage
Sought a new venture
You almost went broke
At times, your spirit gets broken
But you still push on
Move past the doubts
Move past the regrets
Learning from failure
And believing in God
God will provide
You will succeed

The way you move

Move forward with purpose
Not for the sake
Of moving forward
Think forward with vision
Not for the sake
Of thinking forward

There's a way and God will make it

There's a way
And God will make it
There's an algorithm
There's a formula
There's a process
There's a procedure
There's a way
To win is to find how things work
God will make a way

Find your purpose

Be strong and courageous
You will find your purpose
Be strong and courageous
God is bigger than your problems

Find clarity

Be strong and courageous
You will find clarity

Be strong and courageous
You will find clarity

Find the way

Be strong and courageous
You will find the way

You will overcome

Be strong and courageous
You will overcome

Unburden yourself

Be strong and courageous
You will unburden yourself

Fight with faith

Be strong and courageous
Fight with faith

Find your strength

Be strong and courageous
God gives you strength

Brighter days are coming.

You will heal

Be strong and courageous
You will heal

Healing tears

Cry a little, it helps
Use your worries to transform yourself

J o y

There's just something about joy
When the joy comes in the morning
When the sunrise gives you a warm hug
And urges you to smile
To be happy
To be free
To focus on growth
And the values that matter the most
Even joy itself enjoys seeing you rejoice
Being in a state of joy and delight
In my morning prayer, I pray to find joy
To find joy in success and good fortune
To find joy in an unforgiving world
Because there's just something about joy
When the joy comes in the morning

This is the day

I will not waste my time
I will not waste my resources
I will embrace every opportunity
I will try my best to triumph
I will do my best
I will be better
I will be productive
This is the day

I am all ears

Talk to me, I am all ears
I have my worries too
But I love listening to you
I have my doubts too
But I love listening to you
I have my anxieties too
But I love listening to you
I have my fears
I have scars and frustrations too
But I love listening to you
Because listening to you is also part of my self-healing
To remind me that I'm strong
That I have a God bigger than my problems

Whispers from a flower

The flower says
Observe me
I will teach you how to grow
Listen to me
I will teach you how to grow
Mirror me
You too shall grow
I will teach you how to grow
Your mind will be as beautiful as a flower
Your thoughts will be beautiful
Your feelings will be beautiful
And your focus will only be on beautiful things

Destined to win

It's never too far
Winners prepare
And winners prepare well
It's never too much work
Winners plan
And winners plan well
Winners believe they can do all things
For they are strengthened
And designed to win
Are you a winner?
Only time will tell
It's never too late
Winners commit
And winners commit well

Gratitude is everything

Someone wants to be in your position
Don't take your position for granted
Someone wants to occupy your space
Don't take your space for granted
Someone wants what you have
Don't take what you have for granted

Nothing for granted

<u>7 days of gratitude: Day 1</u>
I take nothing for granted
I will be grateful for all I have
For all I receive
For all answered prayers

The journey

<u>7 days of gratitude: Day 2</u>
I will remember my journey
Where I'm coming from
I have come so far
To get to where I am today
I will continue to grow
To focus on my spirituality
And my soulfulness

Learning from failure

<u>7 days of gratitude: Day 3</u>
I have failed so many times
I have fallen so many times
I keep fighting, resilient as ever
Ambitious and determined as ever

Live a little

<u>7 days of gratitude: Day 4</u>
I deserve a treat
I will treat myself
For all my hard work
I will live a little
I will explore
I will travel
I will live a little

Sweet dreams

<u>7 days of gratitude: Day 5</u>
I deserve a good night's sleep
I have worked so hard
I have earned my rest
I go again tomorrow
Chasing my dreams
Making things happen
Making the most of my time

Don't forget your dreams.

Precious time

<u>7 days of gratitude: Day 6</u>
I will take a moment
To realize that time is precious
That time is all I have
I will use my time to grow
To learn
To make things happen
To love and to be loved
I will not waste my precious time

God, family and friends

<u>7 days of gratitude: Day 7</u>
I am grateful for a wonderful God
A God who has blessed me
With family and friends
With a purpose
My God gives me strength
I have faith in my God
I am grateful
I am thankful for each passing day

Pathway to a Dream

<u>Words about sleep and dreams</u>
I seek your comfort, God
I seek your care, God
In need of courage and strength
To walk on this path
This pathway to a dream
However daunting this path may seem
However daunting this path may become
However dark, however trying
I will never walk on this path alone
Even where it feels like I'm all alone
When I lose courage and strength
I will remember the words
"Cast all your anxieties on Him..."

A dream within reach

<u>Words about sleep and dreams</u>
Let whatever
Let whatever is coming to me come to me
I'm sick and tired of
Chasing people now
Who become ghosts later
Chasing dreams now before they become nightmares later
Chasing goals now
Yet find myself drowning tomorrow
In a pool of aimlessness
Believing that whatever happens
Happens for a reason
Tomorrow, I'll find myself
I'll find myself where I belong
Where I will find my reason for being
Where people inspire me to grow
Where dreams are within reach
Where I can accomplish my goals
That is my dream
A dream within reach

Searching for

Words about sleep and dreams
Search right
Search left
Search up
Search down
Search north, search south
Search east, search west
Search above
Search below
Search near
Search far
Search in familiar places
Search in unfamiliar places
For as long as you search with a clear mind
As long as you search with all your heart
There is a guarantee, for sure
You will find what you're looking for

Start

<u>Words about sleep and dreams</u>
Start
Start from somewhere
Before you end up nowhere
Where you're confused
Where things are complicated
Where there's no clarity
Start
Start from somewhere
You will end up there
Where you know your purpose
Where everything makes sense
Where you can reach
Where you have clarity
Until you get there
Start
Start
Start from somewhere
Start today

Borrowed dreams

<u>Words about sleep and dreams</u>
How will I succeed?
Working on these borrowed dreams
How will I commit?
Working on these borrowed dreams
Until I realize my dreams
Success will be mine
I will feel it
Commitment will hold my dreams together
I will feel it

Through sleep, through dreams

<u>Words about sleep and dreams</u>
Had I known that
Through sleep, through dreams
I would understand myself better
Then I would pay
More attention to my dreams
Dreams of the past
The present and of the future
Dreams about many things
Warnings, disappointments, encouragements
Fears, loss, sorrow
Happiness, joy, delight
Light, darkness, destruction
Love, hate, peace, war
All dreams are designed to teach me a lesson
Dreams designed to ignite my attention
So that I pay more attention
To the world around me
And the people around me
So from today
I'll pay more attention to my sleep
I'll pay more attention to my dreams

Wake up

<u>Words about sleep and dreams</u>
Wake up
You have a purpose to fill
Wake up
You have a life to live
Wake up
You have the energy to feel
Wake up
You have more to give
Wake up
You have more to receive
Wake up from your beautiful sleep
God has a purpose for you

Sleep, the architect of dreams

<u>Words about sleep and dreams</u>
Sleep
Refreshing for movers
For getters
For shakers
Those who dream in colour during the day
Those who have visionary dreams at night time
Those who do not waste sleep
By sleeping for the sake of sleeping
They dream about old rivers
Pay attention to their childhood dreams
The dreams of their mother and father
The dreams that frighten them
And the dreams that guide them
Sleep is the architect of their dreams

Loud and clear

Open your eyes and you will see clearly
Listen closely, you will learn something
Exercise your right to express yourself
To express your thoughts and feelings
You can only move forward
If you clear up the confusion
Know your roles and responsibilities
Nothing will pass you by
And nobody will take advantage of you

I have faith

I have faith in you
Because you have faith in yourself
And faith in others
You are the embodiment of faith
A good heart filled with faith
A heart filled with love and kindness
Adventurous, a heart filled with wonder
A heart where prayer lives
Where hope lives
And faith is the keeper of your heart

Death of Kings and Queens

Dear Kings and Queens
Bad attitude

Bad mentality

Short temper
Big ego
Bad friends
Bad decisions
Bad choices
All lead to the death
Of Kings and Queens

I need a win

I need a win
I need a win today
I need a win from somewhere
Anywhere
I want to win
For my efforts
For my determination
For my commitment
For my physical and mental resilience
I need to win
I need a win today
I need a win from somewhere
Anywhere

God is good

<u>God is good</u>
Allow me to take this moment to reflect
To say a little prayer
To put my perspective into place
To say thank you God for today's meal
And for that, we say grace
Allow me to take this moment to reflect
To say a little prayer
To say that I'm thankful
With overwhelming gratitude
Grateful for my friends and family
Allow me to take this moment to reflect
To say a little prayer
May God bless me with a vision
And the reality that follows
Because I believe in God
And God believes in me
God is good

Powerful prayer

<u>God is good</u>
We pray and believe
In whatever language
At whatever time of the day
Prayer has never lost its power
Because God has never stopped hearing
And answering our prayers
Even though we do not always
Receive what we ask for
Because God says no to one prayer
And says yes to another
God's presence is always with us
May we pray to find satisfaction in God?
Pray for things that honour our God
Because prayer has never lost its power

Enough room for God

<u>God is good</u>
Have you ever wondered why?
Why the small problems
We experience this in our daily lives
Often turn into big problems
When we try to fix them on our own
Because we say
"This problem is small; I don't need to bother God."
We forget that those big problems
Were once small problems
And that we are held captive by
These chains of ignorance
These chains of arrogance
Simply because we forget God
Because we don't acknowledge God
Because we think we can do it on our own
Because we don't leave enough room for God
So, may we remember God?
May we acknowledge God?
May we make enough room for God?
Because no problem is bigger than God

The long road ahead

<u>God is good</u>
Take a moment to thank God
For how far you have come
Instead of losing sleep
Over the long road ahead
You see
You will be tested on the long road ahead
Your character will be tested
Your personality will be tested
Your nature will be tested
Your resolve will be tested

You will not believe

You will not believe
How many times I quit
When things got hard
When my knees got planted on the floor
Because I simply had enough
You will not believe
How many times I have failed
When things got tough
When my mind, body and spirit
Could not take it anymore
You will not believe
That I never stopped believing
Believing in God
And believing in myself
I will keep pushing
Praying until something happens

True colours

In that moment of doubt
I see your face on a canvas
Painted in true colours
In that moment of confusion
I see your face on a canvas
Painted in true colours
In moments of fear
Moments of anguish
Moments of discomfort
And moments of frustration
I see your face on a canvas
Painted in true colours

Looking out the window

You were made to grow
To be the change you desire to be
To realize yourself
To look out the window
And see the inevitable change
Not look into a mirror
That reflects existing patterns
Think beyond, create new patterns
Look beyond, see new patterns
You were made to grow
To be the change you desire to be

More than enough

Why settle for less
When your God says
You're more than enough
A God who can open doors for you
Break barriers for you
Lift you up
Build you up
And push you up
For you are not just enough
You are more than enough

Time will heal you

Be brave, time will heal you
Be courageous, time will heal you
Be patient, time will heal you
Be hopeful, time will heal you

Keep the grass short

Keep the grass short
They are not happy with your success
They are not happy with your happiness
They are not happy with your freedom
They are not happy with your stability
They are not happy with your position
They wait to pounce on your mistakes
Such snakes, some people you call friends

Deep silence

I need these moments of deep silence
Alone
Thinking about nothing at all
For a brief moment, switch off the world
Escape my body and
Explore oneself in deep silence
To meditate
To re-energize
To focus on the power of positivity
And harness positive energy
I need these few moments to myself
To embrace my mind, body and soul
I need these moments of deep silence

Grateful

Be grateful
When you receive something you want
Be grateful for what you have
Be grateful
When you receive something you need
Be grateful for what you have
Beyond that
Everything becomes toxic
Too much power, poisonous
Too much ambition, poisonous
Too much pride, poisonous
Too much ego, poisonous
Be grateful for what you receive
Be grateful for what you have

See it coming

Open your eyes
You will see success coming
Open your eyes
You will see failure coming
Open your eyes
You will see loyalty coming
Open your eyes
You will see deception coming
Open your eyes
You will see peace coming
Open your eyes
You will see tension coming
Open your eyes
Seek clarity
Pray for clarity

I love you, my child

I love you, my child
Do not be anxious, do not worry
I see the future in your eyes
A bright and prosperous future
Get your priorities right
And always remember
To put God and family first
To learn is to grow
To sacrifice is to mature
To have a passion, to be passionate
Then all you touch will turn into gold
Everything you touch will prosper
I love you, my child

I love you, my child

Silence the thinking that unsettles your mind

Guide me, God
Shield me, God
Lead me, God
Give me the strength
Give me the wisdom
To silence the thinking
That unsettles my mind
For I seek spirituality
For I seek knowledge
For I seek clarity

Overcome

I faced the dark days
Overcame all the negativity
Away from my mind
Away from my heart
Away from my spirit
Reclaimed my thoughts
Reclaimed my feelings
Reclaimed my soul
My purpose in life, I no longer question
My prayer for peace of mind
My prayer to overcome anxiety
My prayer to overcome depression

Birds will swim, fish will fly

The day I forget my God
Birds will swim, fish will fly
The day I forget my family
Birds will swim, fish will fly
The day I forget my home
Birds will swim, fish will fly
The day I forget myself
Birds will swim, fish will fly
May it never change?
I will remember my God
I will remember my family
I will remember my home
I will remember myself
And most of my days will be glorious
And the birds will fly
The fish will swim

Feeling like myself again

I feel like myself again
My skin fits
I feel like myself again
My personality fits
I feel like myself again
My mentality fits
I feel like myself again
My body fits

Love

<u>Words to keep you focused, there's more to life</u>
Focus on love
You will find that it is a beautiful thing

<u>Words to keep you focused, there's more to life</u>
Focus on love
You will find that it is a beautiful thing

Growth

<u>Words to keep you focused, there's more to life</u>
There's more to life
You will find growth

Faith

<u>Words to keep you focused, there's more to life</u>
Focus on your faith
You will find that it is a powerful thing

Move on

<u>Words to keep you focused, there's more to life</u>
There's more to life
Move on
There's light at the end of the tunnel

Hope

<u>Words to keep you focused, there's more to life</u>
Focus on hope
You will find the push you need

Smile more

<u>Words to keep you focused, there's more to life</u>
There's more to life
You should smile more

Peace

<u>Words to keep you focused, there's more to life</u>
Focus on peace
You will find that it is a refreshing thing

Dream more

<u>Words to keep you focused, there's more to life</u>
There's more to life
You should dream more

Uplifting joy

<u>Words to keep you focused, there's more to life</u>
Focus on joy
You will find that it is an uplifting thing

Be brave

<u>Words to keep you focused, there's more to life</u>
There's more to life
Be brave

<u>Words to keep you focused, there's more to life</u>
There's more to life
Be brave

Comfort

<u>Words to keep you focused, there's more to life</u>
Focus on comfort
You will find that it is a necessary thing

Endure the pain

<u>Words to keep you focused, there's more to life</u>
There's more to life
Endure the pain

Endure the pain

<u>Words to keep you focused, there's more to life</u>
There's more to life
Endure the pain

Forgiveness

<u>Words to keep you focused, there's more to life</u>
Focus on forgiveness
You will find the power to move on

Part of the journey

<u>Words to keep you focused, there's more to life</u>
There's more to life
Loss, failure, pain and suffering are part of the journey

Dreams

<u>Words to keep you focused, there's more to life</u>
Focus on your dreams
You will find your passion
Focus on purpose and meaning
You will find your true self

Win some, lose some

<u>Words to keep you focused, there's more to life</u>
There's more to life
You win some battles, you lose some battles

Win some, lose some

<u>Words to keep you focused, there's more to life</u>
There's more to life
You win some battles, you lose some battles

Healing, resilience

<u>Words to keep you focused, there's more to life</u>
Focus on healing
You will grow in all aspects of your life
Focus on your resilience
You will unlock your positivity

Pushing boundaries

<u>Words to keep you focused, there's more to life</u>
There's more to life
Keep pushing boundaries
Fall and fall again
Fail and fail again
You will overcome
You are enough
There's more to life

See tomorrow

When you see another day
The sun will shine
The wind will blow
Rivers will flow
Birds will fly, fish will swim
But should you not see another day
The sun will still shine
The wind will still blow
Rivers will still flow
Birds will still fly and fish will still swim
But your family and friends will miss you
You will have left a void
Only sweet memories can fill
So be thankful when you see tomorrow

Cheers to peace of mind

Cheers to peace of mind
My mind is at peace
My heart is at ease
I am in a good place
Cheers to peace of mind

Brightened mood

I am in control of myself
I can smile again
I can sleep again
I can dream again
My mood is brightened

I remember

I remember now
What it means to have
An interest in something
What it means to
Enjoy something, to have a passion

I remember now

Appetite for life

My appetite for love is big
My appetite for success is big
My appetite for serenity is big
My appetite for stability is big
Most importantly
My appetite for life is big

Healing rest

I deserve my healing rest
Having learned to overcome stress
I pray for fewer sleepless nights
I pray for more restful nights
I pray for more quiet nights
I deserve my healing rest

On the move

My life story is in motion
I watch it in my head
Seeing myself in places I desire to be
Seeing myself at places I desire to be
My life story is in motion
I am on the move

Full of energy

I am full of energy
Because God gives me strength
My mind is in the right place
My heart is in the right place
To brighter days
I am full of energy

Worthy

I am worthy of love
I am worthy of prosperity
I am worthy of respect
I am worthy of admiration
I feel worthy
I am worthy

Concentrate

I tell myself every morning
Concentrate on happiness
Concentrate on your plans
Concentrate on your actions
Concentrate on the road ahead
Concentrate
Concentrate

It happens

It happens
But don't let it control you
Remember your face
Remember your voice
It's just tension
It's just stress
It's just a disappointment
It's just frustration
It happens
But don't let it control you

Life

There's more to life
There's more to live for
Focus on joy, not suicidal thoughts
Focus on healing, not destructive behaviour
There's more to life
There's more to live for
Choose to live
Choose life

Cheers to happiness

Cheers to happiness
I'm filled with overwhelming joy
I welcome each day
With the brightest smile
For joy comes in the morning

Cheers to success

Cheers to success
Hard work pays off
Smart work pays off
Good work pays off
Consistent work pays off
Resilience pays off
My mind is designed to win
Cheers to success

Cheers to family

Cheers to family
To my support system
My blood, my people
I'm grateful for your support
For your advice
Your attention
Your love
And your thoughtfulness
Cheers to family

Cheers to a good and abundant life

Cheers to a good and abundant life
To more life
Fulfilling life
Abundant life
A good life
Cheers to a fulfilling
Good and abundant life

Cheers to therapy

Cheers to therapy
To the ears that heard my worries
To the hearts that felt my pain
To the voices that said, "It's okay to open up"
And made me feel
That we are in this together
Cheers to that healing journey
Cheers to therapy

Cheers to freedom of expression

Cheers to freedom of expression
I will not hide my thoughts
I will not hide my feelings
Cheers to freedom of expression

Cheers to tranquillity

Cheers to tranquillity
I have travelled on this long journey
I deserve my moments of tranquillity
To only focus on oneself
My mental well-being
My spiritual well-being
And my physical well-being
Cheers to growth
Cheers to tranquillity

Cheers to good health

Cheers to good health
I hope these words find you in good health
Good health looks good on you, I can tell

If you're concealing any pain, I advise you to get some help
I see you're smiling, that's a good sign
Do you know how many muscles it takes to pull off a smile?
I see you're walking
Strolling, marching as a triumphant horse straight from the
battlefield
Do you know what a blessing it is to get off your bed and stand
up on your own two feet?
I see you're on the move
Lifting things up
Pushing things, pulling things
And making things happen
Thanks to good health, today you can walk
Thanks to good health, today you can talk
Above all, we thank God for good health
For God is the doctor who doctors all doctors
When doctors have no one to doctor them
I hope these words find you in good health
I pray that you grow physically, mentally and spiritually
Cheers to good health

Wildflower affirmation 1

I will remember the sweetness of your love for me and my love for you

Wildflower affirmation 2

I will remember not to suppress my pain and rise from the depths of despair

Wildflower affirmation 3

I will remember that the loss of love and the loss of a loved one are beyond my control

Wildflower affirmation 4

I will remember the moments when my heart was filled with pain and questions

Wildflower affirmation 5

I will remember that to heal, I need an abundance of insight and direction

Wildflower affirmation 6

I will remember that the pain of a broken heart and a broken bone can heal

It only takes time

If a broken bone can heal, so can my broken heart

Wildflower affirmation 7

I will remember to give birth to a new me

Wildflower affirmation 8

I will remember to believe in a new and fulfilling life

Wildflower affirmation 9

I will remember to focus on partial and permanent healing

Wildflower affirmation 10

I will remember that others have stood where I stand now

Wildflower affirmation 11

I will remember to turn my tears of pain into tears of gratitude

Wildflower affirmation 12

I will remember that when life spirals down, the wings of hope will carry my devotion

Wildflower affirmation 13

I will remember that anything can happen at any moment. Beyond everything I could have expected, predicted or imagined

Wildflower affirmation
14

I will remember to reset my heart, find forgiveness, learn to smile again, start caring again, start trusting again, start committing again and release my unresolved feelings

Wildflower affirmation 15

I will remember to look back, reflect and transform
I will remember that all the pain and tears will soon just be a memory

Much love to American / Portuguese visual artist, Kristen Palana, inspired by my poem 'Behind the Smile', as an initiative to encourage mental, emotional and spiritual healing.

About the author

Tendai M. Shaba is a Malawian writer, poet, activist and author of Moments to cherish (2020) A Lady in a Yellow Dress (2023) and Living with the Wildflowers (2024). He has officially been involved as an activist in numerous campaigns on mental health awareness, women, girls and youth empowerment, labour and productivity and climate change. You can access more of his work here: http://www.tendaishaba.com/

Acknowledgements

With everything you face
Embrace it with grace
All the tears will wash away in the rain
And all the pain will soon be just a memory
You believe that if a broken bone can heal
Your broken heart can heal too
You know what it means to feel blue
But you are strong and inspired
You are beautiful and admired
Beauty, love, peace and light surround you
As a loss, sadness, fear and anguish do too
You acknowledge all the wildflowers
You accept all the wildflowers
And you find peace living with the wildflowers